5074 0314

IF BOOKS

If An EGG HATCHES...
AND OTHER ANIMAL PREDICTIONS

BY BLAKE A. HOENA

CAPSTONE PRESS
a capstone imprint

Some animals swing in the trees. Others fly or burrow in the earth. Each animal is amazing. But they all follow the laws of nature. Watch closely and you can predict what animals will do. Want to give it a try?

Baby animals enter the world in different ways. Dogs, cats, cows, bats, and other mammals give birth to live babies. Other animals lay eggs. When an egg hatches, what kind of animal might you find?

ANSWER

A baby bird, like a chick,
might pop out of an egg.
Or you could see a reptile
like a snake or a turtle
crawl out. Even insects and
amphibians hatch from eggs!

Playing hide-and-seek with a chameleon would be tricky. This lizard's skin can match the colors around it. Next to leaves, a chameleon turns green. It turns brown next to branches.

What color do you think a desert chameleon would be?

ANSWER

5

Next to rocks and sand, chameleons turn brown, gray, or tan. Camouflage helps chameleons hide from predators and hunt for prey.

Dolphins are mammals. They live in the ocean like fish, but they don't have gills. They breathe with lungs, like people do. A dolphin can hold its breath for a long time.
But what does a dolphin do when it needs a breath of air?

ANSWER

They poke their heads out of the water. A dolphin can breathe using the blowhole on the top of its head. That way, even when most of a dolphin's body is under water, a dolphin can still breathe air.

All summer long, Canada geese live in northern North America. They paddle around lakes and ponds eating plants and bugs. Autumn brings cool weather. Soon the lakes and ponds will be covered in ice. What will the geese do?

ANSWER

They will migrate, or fly south where it's warm. Canada geese migrate to places where they can find food. The geese fly north again in spring when the weather warms.

A deer's hooves help it speed through woods and grasslands. Hunting tigers slip quietly through the jungle on soft, padded paws. River otters spend most of their time in the water. What kind of feet do you think otters have?

ANSWER

River otters have wide, webbed feet. Just like swimming flippers, webbed feet help otters move quickly through water.

Mice and other rodents have long tails and big teeth. In fact, a mouse's front teeth never stop growing! But if the mouse's teeth get too long, it can't open its mouth to eat.

What could a mouse do to keep its teeth trimmed?

ANSWER

They chew! Mice nibble, gnaw, and chew through wood, cloth, and plastic. They can even chew through some kinds of metal! All that chewing keeps rodents' teeth the perfect size.

Fish use their fins to dart and swim through the ocean. Shrimp have lots of little legs to scuttle on the ocean floor. But what about jellyfish? These animals have no legs and no fins, no bones and no muscles! How does a jellyfish get around?

ANSWER

A jellyfish's bell-shaped body opens to let water in. When the jellyfish squeezes its body, the water shoots out again. The moving water pushes the jellyfish where it needs to go.

During the summer, an arctic fox creeps through the brown tundra. These foxes hunt arctic rabbits. The foxes' brown fur helps them sneak up close. But what happens when snow turns the tundra white?

ANSWER

In the winter, an arctic fox's coat turns white. Lucky for arctic rabbits, their fur turns white in winter too!

A brown bear has a mighty hungry belly. After all, it takes lots of food to fill up a bear. In the winter, there are no berries, leaves, bugs, or fish for the bear to eat. What could it do to survive?

ANSWER

In the winter, bears hibernate. They find a safe, warm place to rest until spring. Hibernating saves energy, so bears don't need to search for food.

A plant's leaves soak up sunlight, turning it into the energy the plant needs to grow. Then along hops a grasshopper, nibbling on the plant. A garter snake slithers by and gobbles up the grasshopper. What happens next?

ANSWER

The snake may be eaten by an owl, a fox, or a lynx. They are predators at the top of the food chain, and they all eat snakes.

Imagine eating the same food all day EVERY day! Giant pandas live in Asian mountain forests. They eat bamboo and nothing else. As people cut down the forests, there is less and less bamboo. What do you think will happen to the pandas?

ANSWER

23

As the forests disappear, so do the giant pandas. People have started protecting giant pandas' homes and sheltering the pandas in zoos. Without our help, these endangered animals will become extinct.

Tadpoles hatch from eggs, and did you know that they're actually baby frogs? Eventually their legs sprout and their tails shrink. Then the frogs can hop out of the pond. Soon they will mate with another frog.
What will happen next?

ANSWER

After frogs mate, female frogs will lay eggs. Tadpoles hatch from the eggs, and the frogs' life cycle begins again.

Every animal in nature is important. Imagine if there weren't any predators like wolves. What would happen to the populations of elk and deer?

ANSWER

27

Their populations would grow and grow. If there are too many prey animals like deer, there won't be enough plants and shrubs for food. Then some of the deer would starve. Predators like wolves help keep prey populations from growing too large.

How many answers did you predict correctly? Did you already know a lot about animals or did you learn something new? Animals may do some strange and amazing things. If you watch them closely, you can better understand their habits and learn why each one is important to the natural world.

GLOSSARY

camouflage—a pattern or color on an animal's skin that makes it blend in with the things around it

endangered—at risk of dying out

extinct—no longer living; an extinct animal is one that has died out, with no more of its kind

food chain—a series of plants and animals in which one eats the one below it in the chain

hibernate—to spend winter in a deep sleep; animals hibernate to survive low temperatures and lack of food

life cycle—series of changes an animals goes through during its life

mate—to join together to produce young

migrate—to move from one place to another

population—total number of one kind of animal

predator—an animal that hunts other animals for food

prey—an animal hunted by another animal for food

tundra—a cold area where trees do not grow; the ground stays frozen in the tundra for most of the year

READ MORE

Amstutz, Lisa J. *Polar Animal Adaptations.* Amazing Animal Adaptations. Mankato, Minn.: Capstone Press, 2012.

De la Bédoyère, Camilla. *Biggest and Smallest.* Animal Opposites. Buffalo, N.Y.: Firefly Books, 2011.

Peterson, Megan Cooley. *Look inside a Robin's Nest.* Look Inside Animal Homes. Mankato, Minn.: Capstone Press, 2012.

INTERNET SITES

FactHound offers a safe, fun way to find Internet sites related to this book. All of the sites on FactHound have been researched by our staff.

Here's all you do:

Visit *www.facthound.com*

Type in this code: 9781429687188

Super-cool stuff! Check out projects, games and lots more at www.capstonekids.com

A+ Books are published by Capstone Publishers,
1710 Roe Crest Drive, North Mankato, MN 56003
www.capstonepub.com

Library of Congress Cataloging-in-Publication Data
Cataloging-in-publication information is on file with the Library of Congress.
ISBN 978-1-4296-8718-8 (library binding)
ISBN 978-1-4296-9245-8 (paperback)
ISBN 978-1-62065-191-9 (eBook PDF)

Credits

Jeni Wittrock, editor; Ted Williams, designer; Svetlana Zhurkin, media researcher; Laura Manthe,
    production specialist

Photo Credits

Biosphoto: Jean-Michel Labat, 20; Capstone Studio: Karon Dubke, cover; Dreamstime: Andrea Baldrighi, 16, Bobolok, 9, Chris
Lorenz, 27, Jekaterina Vlassova, 28, Martaposp, 26, Michael Sheehan, 3, Saeid Shahin Kiya, 1; iStockphotos: John Henderson,
18, Kerstin Klaassen, 25, Paul Tessier, 4, Stephen Strathdee, 10; Minden Pictures: Flip Nicklin, 8, Michael & Patricia Fogden,
13; Shutterstock: Creatista, 12, CreativeNature, 14, Dani Vincek, 24, dirkr, 6, Login (question background), throughout, Marty
Wakat, 7, moomsabuy, 2, Nataliia Melnychuk, 11, Oksana Perkins, 19, Olga Khoroshunova, 23, Peter Wollinga, 21, Roger
Jones, 22, Sebastian Duda, 5, Stephen Meese, 29, ttueni, 15, Wild Arctic Pictures, 17

Note to Parents, Teachers, and Librarians

This If Book uses full color photographs and fun text to introduce K-2 nature concepts in an interactive, predictive format. *If an
Egg Hatches . . . And Other Animal Predictions* is designed to be read aloud to a pre-reader or to be read independently by
an early reader. Photographs help listeners and early readers understand the text and concepts discussed. The book encourages
further learning by including the following sections: Glossary, Read More, and Internet Sites. Early readers may need assistance
using these features.

Printed in the United States of America in North Mankato, Minnesota.
042012   006682CGF12